BUILDING YOUR ADVERTISING BUSINESS

BUILDING YOUR ADVERTISING BUSINESS

A Complete
Guide to Boost
Your Billings

DAVID M. LOCKETT

NTC Business Books
a division of *NTC Publishing Group* • Lincolnwood, Illinois USA

Published by NTC Business Books, a division of NTC Publishing Group.
©1989 by NTC Publishing Group, 4255 West Touhy Avenue,
Lincolnwood (Chicago), Illinois 60646-1975 U.S.A.
Manufactured in the United States of America.
Library of Congress Catalog Card Number: 88-63392

9 0 ML 9 8 7 6 5 4 3 2 1

Contents

Introduction

Advertising agencies of all sizes and in all locations have a product to sell: talent, media, public relations, marketing, sales promotion—and we sell all of them, some of them, or most of them. The ability to market effectively and communicate to the public a client's product or service is what we, as agencies, are all about.

Fine, we all understand that. But, in our concern for marketing, what we sometimes fail to realize is that without clients we can't be in the advertising agency business. NO CLIENTS . . . NO AGENCY! It's that simple.

Fortunately, most of us are smart enough to know this agency fact of life. But the big question that then surfaces is "How do we get new business?"

Some agencies are fortunate enough to get their new business because of their highly visible and exemplary work. Potential advertisers are drawn because they want the same kind of treatment or high caliber creative work for their product. Such agencies are often called by an advertiser and are the ones often mentioned in the pages of *Advertising Age* as pitching this or that account.

An excellent way for a small agency to build a good reputation, and a solid business, is to specialize. The agency can become expert at one type of advertising, such as direct mail, or at serving one type of client.

Using his background as an artist, a Chicago man opened a one-man shop specializing in advertising and public relations for the fashion business. In particular, he developed a good working relationship with representatives of fashion publications. Understanding their requirements for advertising art, he can produce illustrations and layouts that meet the needs of both the client and the publication where the ad will appear.

But the success stories aside, the problem of getting new business is as crucial and continual for larger advertising agencies as it is for smaller ones. The difference is that the smaller or medium-sized agency (up to $25 million in billing) must work harder to acquire new accounts.

That's the reason for this book. As a partner of a small industrial/consumer advertising agency in Chicago, I found my account executives wanting to know more about the art of getting new business. At a small agency, we were all (top management, creative, account management) responsible for getting new business (a regrettable policy, as you will soon learn). I had my ways and they worked. But after a time I became increasingly curious about how larger agencies pursue and capture new business.

To my horror, I found little material on the subject. I learned later that lectures on "getting new business" occurred in a vacuum. Most agency executives who addressed themselves to the subject did so in very general terms and often asked that notes and recording devices not be used during their talks. Even the manuals or textbooks devoted to the advertising agency business offer at most a chapter or two of light discussion on acquiring new business. News clippings are scarce as well.

I contacted many agency executives to ask, "What information do you have on getting new business?" The invariable reply: "Not too much." The lack of existing material became a challenge to me. I started calling a few friends I know in the business. They in turn told me to call or write people they knew who had a unique approach or a unique plan for getting new business leads. I soon became aware that whatever information did exist on new business existed via a gigantic national grapevine. A lot of people were afraid to talk to me for fear they would divulge some secret formula that only they knew about.

So I took a different approach. I listed many of the suggestions that had come my way. Then when I approached an agency executive responsible for new business (usually the president of the agency), I'd tell him or her, "I have a list of tactics used by agencies in getting new business. Would you concur with their usage or not? Does your agency use the same tactics? If not, why not? And last, can you give me any suggestions that are different or unique?"

It worked! Once I got the agency executive talking about getting new business, picking his or her brain for new suggestions was relatively easy.

I learned two valuable lessons: First, most if not all advertising agencies use the same techniques. There really is no mysterious and secret recipe that will produce fantastic new business results overnight. The formula is BASIC! Each agency is essentially employing the same new business machinery as the next agency, although some emphasize different suggestions than others. It's a matter of what works better for whom.

Second, I learned that the LEAD is the MOST IMPORTANT of all the new business processes. Before you can research a prospect or talk to a prospect you must have a viable LEAD. You can spend your life talking and writing to people and never produce a lead to a prospective account. Generally, a lead is important information about a company or corporation that is seeking an advertising agency. However, to go beyond that definition, a LEAD in this book means important news that you are privy to first.

I have attempted to share with you nearly three years of constant digging that I had to do to get the answers for my own agency. I won't bore you with success stories and the vast sums of money generated by the suggestions incorporated in this book. Suffice it to say the "road map" has been tested and can take you to your destination: new business LEADS.

I have tried to keep each chapter simple and clear. In some cases, I have elaborated, but most of the time I have provided you with pure basics. Getting overly technical and instructive, I think, would only be confusing. The sooner you grasp the basic ways of getting new business leads, the sooner you can get new business for your agency.

Maybe you can use the entire contents of this book to your benefit. And, then again, maybe you'll find that only a couple of the plans or suggestions in the book will work effectively for you. You will be the judge. Only you can determine what will or will not work. Take from this book what you need.

In this era of mega-mergers in the advertising business, most of the agencies you read about have national, or even global, client lists. Each account brings in hundreds of thousands of dollars.

"It's our policy to offer free consultations to prospective clients," said one agency executive. "Last week, we spent a couple of hours with a guy who, it turned out, wanted to spend $4,000. We turned it down. We can't afford to do business like that."

However, that same man recalled that when he began his career in advertising, "I would start on the top floor of the Merchandise Mart in Chicago, and call on every single showroom. I'd offer to do any kind of advertising job for them, from designing a poster to doing a mailing piece. When I finished my calls at the Merchandise Mart, I'd go over to the Furniture Mart. Eventually, I got some business.

"Today it still takes that kind of dedication, maybe more. The only other alternative is to marry the boss's daughter, but I wasn't smart enough to think of that!"

The one chapter you won't find here is "Determination and Hard Work." The way I see it is that if you don't have those or the desire for them, all the suggestions in this book are worthless. This book and determination and hard work go hand in hand.

D.M.L.

1 Why New Business?

Agencies need new business for two very important reasons: to survive and to grow. There is an unverified statistic that puts the life expectancy of a new account at approximately eight years. Although we all know of cases where the client/agency relationship has lasted for as long as thirty years and, in some cases, as little as six months, if you accept the eight-year life span theory, then you know that every seven-and-a-half years you're going to have to actively seek new business to replace that which the experts say you are going to lose.

But there are other more important reasons we need new business. Take one of the two categories already noted—survival. Let's face a fact of life . . . no account is FOREVER. Even if you have an account now that your company acquired when Abe Lincoln was a teenager, you cannot be sure that account will stay forever.

Accounts move on for various reasons. The biggest reason is that the rapport between the agency and the client has diminished. This can be caused by poor account management by the agency personnel. It can be caused by below-standard creative work. Or it can be caused by a severe lack of trust on the part of the client toward the agency, a cause often referred to as the "personality gap problem."

There are other reasons why accounts move on. There is the merger or acquisition problem that occurs when your account is bought by a larger company. If you are lucky, the merger will result in your client maintaining its autonomy, thus operating as freely as it did before it was purchased. In this case, you have a good chance of keeping the business. But the probability of the client's advertising going to another agency—because the purchasing company wants a change—is very real.

Then there is the problem of a change in personnel. Your client may hire a new chief operating officer or a new director of advertising. New people often make changes that they believe are in the best interest of the company. The elimination of your agency may be one of those changes. Result: lost account!

Finally, there is the "going out of business" problem, which can result when the client stops the production and distribution of the product for which you are doing the advertising. Or an entire company can close its doors and go out of business for economic reasons.

The bottom line is that we agencies need new business to maintain our revenues, to stay healthy. After all, it takes only a phone call or a letter from the client to the agency head to inform him or her of imminent trouble.

Let's suppose you have four accounts and your total billing for these accounts is $1,000,000. Half of this comes from one account. Let's also suppose you have a staff of nine people. With the $1,000,000 in billing, you can comfortably pay your monthly overhead and still put a few bucks in the bank. Everything is running smoothly and you're at the point of getting ready for the annual agency Christmas cocktail party. On the morning of December 5, your $500,000 client (one-half of your billing) calls the head of the agency and informs him or her that for one reason or another the agency is going to lose the account. Wow! In thirty days, or by January 5, the agency will have to cut three to four people from the staff and make other awkward changes. Merry Christmas!

Several agency staffers are notified and panic runs deep within the agency. There is no excuse for this. New business could have spared this little agency its grief.

Now let's talk about *growth*. Advertising agencies are all eager to grow if only to increase employee take-home salary. New accounts can spur this growth, depending, of course, on the profitability of the account. But the benefits of agency growth go be-

2 Who Should Be Responsible?

If you had the time, the money, and the patience to survey a wide selection of advertising agencies of different sizes and capabilities to find out who is responsible for handling new business, you'd be stunned at the results. Nine times out of ten, the president of the agency is solely responsible for following up leads and meeting prospective new accounts. In the larger agencies, the responsibility is generally shared by a select few upper-echelon agency executives. These executives frequently wine and dine people, mostly senior media representatives, who may now and then drop the name of an advertiser looking to make a change. But for the most part, the responsibility of new business rests on the shoulders of the agency president.

The belief commonly held is that the president knows more about the agency than anyone else, has more time to entertain a prospective new account, has the sort of title or responsibility within the agency to make an immediate impression on the prospect, and has the authority to make promises or statements of fact that will win the account over without having to seek high command approval. For the most part this is all true. The president of the agency does have the needed talent to charm a new account into the agency.

However, common practice is not necessarily correct practice. Today more and more advertising agencies are changing their policies with respect to the president's role in new business. Agencies across the country are just beginning to realize the necessity of inaugurating a new business department or establishing a better ongoing new business discipline. In the past, the president and a select inner group were considered management and the rest of the agency staff considered clerks. This attitude has changed slowly over the years, particularly in the last decade. Now the chief executive officer is called on to manage and control day-to-day activities of the company. That is not to say that the chief executive officer isn't important to the new business effort anymore, but rather that his or her management function is more in demand. As a result, more members of the agency staff are becoming involved in soliciting new accounts and following up leads.

This brief explanation, however, doesn't answer the question, "Who *should* be responsible for new business?"

Start by remembering one very important phrase: NEW BUSINESS IS EVERYONE'S BUSINESS. Write it down, put it on your bulletin board, memorize it. Never forget it. By involving every employee of the agency, from the receptionist to the president, you will produce a harmony that will pay off immeasurably. But before you start sending memos around to staffers, there are several points you should understand.

First, one individual should be solely responsible for the new business activity. No matter how many people are ultimately involved, there should be one "quarterback" to coordinate the agency's new business efforts. That person can be an account executive or the executive vice president. Whoever is chosen should have a thorough knowledge of the agency, its history, its policies, its people, and its strong and weak points. More important, the new business leader should have charm, personality, and the ability to take discouragement along with success. The chosen person should have the character to take upsets maturely but still remain open and genial. And the new business person must be able to *sell*. This person, once chosen, should coordinate new business activities with the chief executive officer on a day-to-day or week-to-week basis.

If you are an agency staff member and want the job, be absolutely sure you have the talents required. If you believe you have the skills, then prepare a new business plan and present it to management. Convince management of the need to create a new business department and the desirability of relieving the president of this task. Or, if you are the chief executive officer of

Lead lists. You will want to file the various lists you have generated here as a backup measure. Lists are made up of: reps/salespeople, directories, friends, family, doctors, lawyers, accountants, and bankers. (Note: you may also add members of associations, clubs, and organizations. See Chapter 11.) Add any other lists that are important to your lead-getting process.

Active prospects. These are files established and maintained separately for each prospect that is actively engaged in reviewing your agency. For example, if a prospect has asked for a presentation, the prospect is active in the sense of selecting you as the advertising agency of record. Therefore, any correspondence in or out, plus memos you have on this prospect should be gathered and put into a separate file with the name of the prospect affixed. These files should be organized alphabetically. Should the potential prospect not become an account, you will place the file in a separate space marked "Prospect Inactive."

Inactive prospects. This is a designated space to place an active prospect file after it has been determined that the prospect is not actively interested in retaining the agency. This is not a graveyard. These files should be maintained because, as you will see, the agency they hire instead of you may not last long or the prospect may alter the direction of the company, thus making it an active prospect again.

Clips. This file should be established to maintain clippings of ads, news releases, or other valuable printed information that may assist you in developing leads.

Follow-up book. Remember the three-ring notebooks discussed earlier? If you recall, one three-ring book is for newsletters (inserted randomly or specifically tabbed, whichever you prefer). Another one is for follow-up. Here's how it works. Tab your three-ring binder with a tab for each month of the year. Every time you make a new contact with a lead, do the following: If, for instance, the prospect shows absolutely no desire to meet with you or further the conversation about your agency, mark your lead card accordingly and place it in the prospect inactive section of your card file. (Do this only if you think pursuit is futile at this time).

If, however, you are asked to call again, or are invited to meet personally with the lead, then write the prospect a letter to recapitulate your conversation or correspondence, make a copy of the letter, and place it in your follow-up notebook behind the tab marked for the month you are to get back to the lead. Place a copy in your correspondence out file as well. You'd be surprised how easy this procedure is. From then on, you can place the letter behind any monthly tab depending on further steps you have to take to keep abreast of the prospect's interest in the agency and the work you are required to do to get the account. Without this simple follow-up procedure, your prospect/lead organization can quickly fall into disarray.

On the front of your letters mark in red the complete phone number of your prospect, including the area code or extension number. Next to the prospect's name note the secretary's first and last name. By knowing the secretary's name, you will increase your chances of talking to the prospect again when you are due to call back. Secretaries are one of your most important assets. If you chat casually with them and act personably, you increase your chances of getting your letters placed promptly on your prospect's desk or getting through to the prospect on the phone when you call.

When you follow up, be sure you note everything you said or accomplished. Your notes might read, for example:

Called 10/12/88. Out of town. CB (call back) 10/20/88.

Called 10/20/88. Prospect would like profile on agency.

Profile sent 10/20/88. CB 10/30/88.

What next? Work your follow-up notebook entries diligently. But, if after you have made a concerted effort to arrange a meeting, or the prospect has advised you that they are going to review another agency, or the prospect's positive attitude turns negative, remove your follow-up letter from the follow-up notebook and place it in your correspondence out file. By doing this you'll keep your follow-up notebook free of deadwood, thus allowing you to concentrate on more active prospects. If your follow-up ing or not right for you, then merely collate a package of the materials previously described and mail it to everyone on your list. If your material is well-written and easily understood, you should see the results shortly.

Follow up your initial mailing occasionally with simply written letters informing your "house list" about current agency developments or examples of how a particular friend or member of the family provided a lead that was especially advantageous for you to have. You may wish to accompany these follow-up letters with examples of current agency work.

After a while you will be able to judge who will or will not be cooperative or valuable to your new business effort.

What about remuneration? That depends on you and your agency. Will those on your list feel insulted if you give them money or tickets to an important event or an evening out? Will your agency foot the bill? You be the judge. But be careful. Check with the agency's attorney first, to be sure you *can* offer remuneration. Some new business people do pay for leads that produce a new account. But again, you and you alone can better determine the losses or benefits if money passes hands.

One last point: When you explain what it is you want your "house list" to do, be sure you make them aware and conscious of their own associations and acquaintances. They are to be sure to keep their ears and eyes open for important business information. Don't just say, "Call when you get a lead." They may not know what a lead is or how to recognize a genuine lead. Be very patient and clear.

The story of Aunt Tessie is instructive. She learned while playing bridge with her next-door neighbor one day that the neighbor's son had just become president of his company. How Aunt Tessie's neighbor raved about her son the president! Aunt Tessie remembered what her friend said, got the name of the corporation, its principal location, and an idea of the corporation's products. Aunt Tessie made a phone call to her nephew that night and a lucky agency new business executive got a good lead and a great entrée to the prospect.

You never know who knows whom. And you never know what someone may hear that is important for you to know, until you educate your friends and family on how to pick up hints for new business leads for you.

6 Your Banker, Lawyer, and Accountant

When a company or a corporation gets started, who do the principals approach first? The professionals: a lawyer for legal reasons; an accountant to keep the books straight; and a banker for lines of credit, and, of course, a place to put the corporation's money. None of the three professionals in this chapter need their functions explained. They all, singularly and collectively, play a major role in business. And they know what's going on before anyone else.

If you have been using your personal lawyer or accountant or banker just for his or her professional services, then read on. These men and women can help you by providing tips about business developments that by our terms are definitely leads. They can alert you to activities within the business community that are so fresh that it may be months before the information becomes public. A note of warning, however. Remember that each member of this highly professional group has an ethical code that he or she must follow strictly. Privileged information or information told by a person to a lawyer, an accountant, or a banker is not divulged for any reason whatsoever until it is ethically safe to do so. Don't make a fool of yourself by constantly "bugging" any of your professionals for information. Let them come to you first and always. It's that simple and that safe. If you push or, worse, offer money or gratuity to any of them, you'll find yourself damaging your relationships and possibly losing their services as well. You may even get an ugly reputation in professional and business circles.

So what do you do? If you are acquainted personally with any of the "magic three," you're one step ahead of most. Most agency executives call upon their attorneys, accountants, and bankers only when it is necessary. After all, you won't call your lawyer to ask him or her to help you make a media decision. Nor would you any of the other professionals on your list to help you determine the color of paper stock for your new letterheads. Frankly there's no reason or need to call them unless you have a specific problem in their specific area. But you are going to have to become better acquainted with all of them.

If you are the new business executive of the agency, but are not involved in the hard-core management of the agency, it is advisable for you to meet the agency's lawyer(s), accountant (that's the external accountant), and bank officer through a meeting arranged by the president of your agency. He or she should do it gladly in light of the potential outcome of such a meeting.

After you have been properly introduced, arrange to meet with each member of your professional group privately. The best way is through entertainment. Don't attempt to conduct a recruiting session at their offices because professionals will be too easily distracted. The point of your meeting will be lost in the welter of their daily routine. By the same token, don't have a meeting at the agency because *your* routine will get in the way. Take them to dinner or meet with them after work (which is always best) and have a drink.

Once with the professional, be frank! These people deal in facts and frank conversation every day of their lives. They're never comfortable with abstracted, idealistic types. Lawyers, accountants, and bankers often have a very limited idea of how our agency business works. They think we and Hollywood go together. The whole idea is to convince them that we function as true businesspeople. And you must not only convince them of this but also that you need to work with them in order for you and your agency to succeed. (These observations apply to the new business executive and to the president of the agency. Whichever you are, you must gain these professionals' confidence in you and your agency.)

Once trust has been established, prepare an agency review. Have samples of your work available to show. Invite each of your professionals to the agency to see samples, meet your people, and, in general, go through the same pace you would put a prospective account through. But do one important, additional thing: Educate them about why companies advertise and how you as an agency function to meet the needs of these companies. Leave nothing to chance. Pretend you are dealing with a fifth grader when explaining the many workings of the agency. Don't talk down to them, of course, but take them by the hand. After all, the more they know about you, your agency functions, and why companies need advertising agencies, the better informed your professionals will be and the better they can help you.

It is advisable to maintain a list incorporating names, addresses, and phone numbers of your professional group. This list should always include your *personal* attorney, accountant, and banker. (Yes, give them the agency tour as well). This list merely provides you with an easy reference for writing or calling.

Stay in touch with your professionals frequently, but not to the point of being a pest. Be low-key in your pursuit. Try to remember the working situation these people face every day as far as business developments are concerned. Here is a brief list of events they may be privy to:

1. New businesses
2. Patents for new products
3. Business expansion
4. Mergers
5. Services for new, key executives
6. Membership on boards of directors
7. Transactions of all kinds
8. Financing

When your group gains confidence in you and your sincerity as a businessperson, you can expect the benefits of an ongoing relationship—new leads to very interesting business opportunities.

◤ Getting the Most from Clients

The title of this chapter came up during a lecture and discussion with advertising professionals concerning new business when the speaker became abundantly aware that his audience didn't know a thing about what he was talking about. In response to this statement, most at the lecture, if not all, replied, "We know clients are important to us, but how do we go about getting new product assignments?" New product assignments are not what the speaker was referring to and not what this chapter refers to, either.

As we've said, it is a proven fact of agency life that all clients have acquaintances, friendships, and business relationships that could be important. Take your client associations a step further. It is conceivable your clients have relatives in key decision-making positions at companies that could be potential accounts for you. But few new business executives ever bother to pursue this form of contact. Often, advertising executives are so busy making their clients happy, fulfilling their needs and wishes, that they forget that clients are people who have excellent contacts, too.

There have been cases when the advertising manager or the marketing manager of a client company came from another company or the marketing manager of a client company came from another company or sometimes from another agency. He or she can be instrumental in arranging for the new business executive of the agency to meet important people at his or her former company with the possibility of getting new accounts.

This sort of "new business" activity goes on every day by the few who know how to get leads.

So how do you use these client contacts? First, make absolutely sure you and the client are on good terms. Check with your account people on the account to be sure there is no tension brewing. Needless to say, if there is tension between the account and the agency, there certainly won't be an opportunity to approach the account on this subject until the current awkwardness is cleared up.

Next, be sure the client is paying his or her bills on time. Make sure there is no money overdue before you approach the prospect.

These warnings out of the way, compose a letter to the client asking for a small portion of his or her time. Be sure you inform the client that the matter you wish to discuss has nothing to do with the management of the account. (See Appendix A, Example 9.)

Sometimes clients get alarmed when they receive letters from the agency that have nothing to do with the existing business relationship. That's why the sample letter uses such phrases as "our agency is proud to have you as an account," or, "the subject concerns a mutual opportunity."

Follow up your letter with a phone call as promised. At the time of your phone call, arrange to meet somewhere other than the client's office, say for lunch or dinner. Getting the client away from his or her business environment will allow for more relaxed thinking and potentially some good advice—even leads.

Let's stop for a moment to clarify a point. If you are the new business executive of the agency, try to have the client session with the president of the client company. You (your agency) may very well be working with the president. If so, all the better. If not, make a point of getting to the chief executive officer.

If, again, you are the new business executive but not assigned to the account on a working basis, then see the account executive first. Tell the account person what your intentions are and what you want to achieve. Let the account person explain what is going on with the brand manager, or the ad manager, or whomever the agency makes client contact with. Don't forget to mention to the account executive that you will be approaching the brand manager or the ad manager as well.

But, by no means, should anyone approach the account for the purpose of gaining new business information except *you*. An attempt brought on by the account executive could prove to be negative. Most accounts don't want the agency executive who is responsible for their business to be looking around for new business. They get the feeling, deservedly, that they are being cheated or slighted in respect to the work that needs to be done in *their* behalf.

Let's get back to your client. By now, he or she is curious to hear what you have to say. After all, you've sent a letter that said little by way of specifics. Then you called him or her for lunch or dinner, again saying very little.

At this point, *get* to the point. Tell the client that growth is as important to you as it is to him or her. Growth, however, depends on two main ingredients for agencies: good work that gets attention and sales pursuit of new accounts. Who can better help the agency gain knowledge of new accounts than a client putting in a good word? Tell the client you would like him or her to list, mentally, friends, family members, and business associates (suppliers, too)—people he or she feels you could talk to about their advertising business. Better, ask if *he* or *she* wouldn't mind approaching these people via a letter or a phone call to request they talk to you.

Unfortunately, most people who read this believe the procedures are easier to read about than to actually accomplish. Too bad! They're missing out on a good thing. Make sure *you* don't assume your client will think you're an idiot and fire you.

Most clients (especially presidents) believe they invented the word "shrewd." Most top-line executives think they concocted the perfect formula for success. Because they are where they are today they're convinced they got that way by being *shrewd*. Therefore, you write a letter that is elusive to your client. You phone in a polite way and you reveal nothing and you request a get-together . . . away from the business domain. You have just sparked the business qualities of opportunism and challenge. Of course, he or she is going to meet you. It's too intriguing not to!

At lunch or dinner, the client is all ears. As you tell him or her you need advice and help, you bring out the authority figure in him or her. And, as you continue, in your humble way, he or she instinctively feels like a mentor—primed to help, eager to help, and egotistically wanting to help. If not, he or she will feel like a failure or a nobody. The client is committed mentally. No chief executive who has an ego wants followers to think he or she can't be of assistance.

Most high-level businesspeople are top people because they are sensitive, talented, and highly capable individuals. Always treat your clients with a great deal of respect and truth. If you want something that makes good business sense and you won't be wasting the time of the individual, then go after it. You'll be further ahead in new business because you made use of this resource.

8 Magazines and Newspapers

If you're like most agency executives, you already have more to read than you have time for. Just the same, keeping abreast of current business situations is very important in acquiring new business leads. If, however, you know what to read or what to look for while reading, you can make your task much more manageable. Don't run out and enroll in a speed reading course unless you have some fanatical desire to devour half a library. The suggestions here are intended to sharpen your skills and to educate you on how to consume a quantity of relevant information about potential new accounts.

First, there are very few general interest publications that will be of specific help. *People* magazine, for example, is an excellent publication and a lot of fun to read, but if offers very little in the way of current business developments that will help you obtain new business. You could list several hundred other consumer publications that are chock-full of interesting tidbits of information, exceptionally well-written fiction, and loads of "how to" articles. But these publications seldom announce important business happenings.

There are a couple of exceptions, however. Since these publications' livelihoods depend on advertising, you may want to analyze the ads to determine which are, in your estimation, poorly done or lacking in effective communication.

First, let's identify the publication groups that will do you the most good. Remember, you and only you know the strengths of your agency. Whatever you read in this chapter should be tailored to meet your agency's needs.

There are essentially three main groups of publications of interest to the person searching for new business leads: business, daily news, and general interest. By far the most important category for lead-gathering is the business publication group. Second in importance is the daily news group, and, last, the general interest group.

Within the business group are publications that are important enough that you should acquire subscriptions. These include *Advertising Age*, the *Wall Street Journal*, and *AdWeek*. *Advertising Age* needs little introduction to the advertising person. As the leading publication for the advertising trade, its contents are chiefly concerned with news within the advertising community, as well as events in the media and business communities.

AdWeek is the other important advertising trade publication. This magazine has strong regional bureaus, which gather news from all parts of the country.

Likewise, the *Wall Street Journal* needs little introduction. The *Journal*, as it is commonly referred to, addresses itself to important daily activities in business, finance, industry, and government.

As well as national business publications, most cities now have local business weekly papers, such as *Crain's Chicago Business* or the *San Jose Business Journal*. These publications cover smaller businesses in their geographical areas.

In addition to advertising trade journals, track down any trade publications for the industries your agency serves. These may range from *Women's Wear Daily*, the well-known daily newspaper for the women's apparel trade, to a small monthly bulletin that covers a single aspect of a certain trade. There are hundreds of trade publications, and nearly all of them contain valuable information about business developments, people in the industry, and general trends.

There are certainly more publications to consider within the general business information arena. Other highly regarded publications to look through are *U.S. News & World Report*, *Time*, *Forbes*, *Fortune*, *Business Week*, and *Newsweek*.

The next important category is daily news. Depending on

your business objectives, you should receive several of the larger metropolitan newspapers such as the *New York Times*, the *Chicago Tribune*, the *Denver Post*, the *Miami Herald*, the *Times-Picayune* (New Orleans), the *San Francisco Herald*, the *Los Angeles Times*, the *Dallas Morning News* or *Times Herald*, the *Houston Chronicle*, and the *Atlanta Journal-Constitution*. Other papers such as the *Milwaukee Journal* or the *Louisville Times* may be of direct importance to you as well. All daily news publications are important, but you must determine *which* of the dailies are of most benefit to you.

Make a list of publications in all categories, including any general interest publications, that are important for you to read. If you're unsure about your needs, go to your local library and spend a few hours reading magazines and newspapers to determine which publications will provide you with the best information. Or, if you prefer, go to the *Standard Rate and Data Service* listings of business, consumer, and daily news publications. SRDS has a directory for each category. If, by chance, your agency doesn't have the SRDS directories, your library should.

You should be on the lookout for the following:

Executive promotions. Executives such as advertising directors, marketing directors, and presidents who are newly appointed should be noted. Most new executives are like owners of a new house. No matter how attractive the wallpaper is in the living room, they'll want to change it. To feel comfortable within their own new surroundings, just-promoted executives will—in all probability—make changes. Those changes may include anything from the lamp on the desk to the advertising agency presently working on the account. Make a point of sending a newly appointed executive a congratulatory letter. Who knows . . . your letter may prompt an inquiry. But by all means stay in touch.

Executive vacancies. A small blurb in *Industrial Packaging* may inform you that the marketing director or the ad manager or even the president has departed from a particular company, and a replacement is being sought. Check occasionally to see if the position has been filled. Once it has, you have a new name to write to or call for an appointment.

New technology. An executive from an agency specializing in direct mail advertising noted that "technology has changed our business more than any other thing. We use computers in our office, but more important are the tools available to do a better job for our clients. For example, the printing presses we use today make it possible for us to produce large volumes of mailing pieces quickly and cheaply.

"In order to do our job well, we must spend a great deal of time keeping up with new advances in our industry. Some of our clients think they know everything about the advertising business, but all they're really concerned about is how much it costs. It's up to us to get the job done."

New products. More than likely there already is an agency working for the company producing the new product. But don't be surprised if you make an inquiry and find out that the company making the new product is going to interview agencies to handle the product, or new products in general. Here's another trick you may wish to consider. If there is a press release concerning a new product, then obviously everyone knows about it. Should your inquiry to the manufacturer produce no tangible results, contact the competition. Tell them your story and how they can benefit by using your agency in developing marketing and advertising for a similar product, hence allowing the contact to get his or her fair share of the market.

As an example, if you just read that the XYZ Company is introducing a product that will, let's say, eliminate snow from the driveway in one-third the time other conventional products do, and you can't get in to see the ad manager of XYZ Company, then get busy and list the names of companies that have the machinery and capability to come up with a similar device. Contact them and give them your pitch. After all, wouldn't you want to market wonder devices, too? Or would you prefer your competition to "get a leg up" in the marketplace? In the same vein, wouldn't you as the marketing director who just learned the competition introduced a new snow eliminating device want to work with companies or people who can help you gain the most share of market possible with your own version of the product?

Accounts looking. This is an awkward category since by

rights it should be the first thing to look for. By the time an announcement is made that a company or corporation is looking for a new agency, however, it's generally too late. The account has a list they're going to work from, or they have already chosen an agency. Or, frankly, what could happen is that two thousand agencies responded and you're two thousand and one. Don't let "sorry, but not interested," deter you. Contact the company anyway. You may well be invited to talk to make a presentation, but take some initiative in this regard. An awful lot of agencies have acquired accounts by going ahead in the face of a rebuff.

Mergers or acquisitions. A company or corporation that has been newly acquired or has been merged into another may well be headed for an agency shake-up by the acquiree. Contact a senior executive at the parent company and ask if there will be a review of the advertising program. If so, make your intentions known.

A loss in earnings announcement. Read these releases carefully. More than likely the loss in profits may be due to a significant drop in sales. If so, the company taking the loss may feel a whole new marketing and advertising approach will be necessary to upgrade the profitability of the losing product. You will want to communicate your expertise and convince the company that you have the capabilities to re-market the product and advertise it. A word of caution: If possible, try the product or analyze the service first. If the product doesn't work, or tastes bad, and the makers of that product are not willing to make constructive changes, then don't go after the prospect. If you do go ahead and are *unfortunate* enough to get the account, it is likely that all the smart marketing and advertising in the world won't change consumer attitudes and you'll be left with a product failure along with an aggravating and short-lived relationship. A great ad man once said, "If it tastes bad, the public will never buy it again." Why be the agency responsible for consumer distaste?

New companies or corporations. For the most part, these announcements indicate virgin territory. Contact them. They may grow slowly at first, but if you get the new "McDonald's" of companies, you could be well on your way to additional profits and a solid account in no time. But be careful. New companies are short on money and long on motivation. Watch your receivables for at least a year or two.

Again, once you have developed a list of publications that you will read weekly and once you have extricated the information you require, get to the business of contacting the companies or individuals you've noted. It's advisable that you keep handy the *Standard Directory of Advertisers*, published annually by the National Register Publishing Company and available either by geographical breakdowns or by product categories. They also provide a weekly update service as well. Again, your library will have a copy should the agency not keep one on file.

Keep a record of your correspondence and update it frequently. Sooner or later all this information you're gathering will bear fruit—but you must stay organized; otherwise fresh leads will evaporate before you know it.

One further caveat. Be very careful about contacting a company or advertiser who in your estimation is producing "junk" advertising. I once had occasion to call a company that, I thought, produced a poorly executed ad. Being familiar with the product, I plunged ahead and miraculously got the president of the company on the phone. "Hello, Mr. So-and-so. My name is . . ., and I'm with the XYZ Agency. I saw your ad today in the ABC publication and thought I'd give you a call." "Oh!" said the president, "what can I do for you?" I proceeded to tell the president that in my *professional* estimation the ad was done very badly. However, our agency would quickly repair the situation once appointed the agency of record. A terrible silence followed and finally the president said, "Bad ad, huh? Well, you see, my 20-year-old daughter wrote and produced the ad and, frankly, I like it. Thanks for your call, but I'm afraid we're quite satisfied at this time." And he abruptly hung up.

Two months later I was having a drink with a close friend who happened to operate his own ad agency. "What's happening, Chuck?" I inquired. "How's everything going?" "Great," responded my friend. "Couldn't be better. We just signed up the XYZ account. You should have seen the stuff they were previously running. It was ghastly. But I got the president of the company on the phone and somehow got an appointment. We talked and he asked me what I thought about the ad he'd been running. I avoided the question like the plague but in turn asked him if he liked the ads and, more importantly, if the ads were working. Fortunately, he hated the ads and they weren't working. So I showed him our material and we came away with the account. Funny thing, every time someone called him and told him the ads were bad he'd have nothing further to do with the caller. You'd think his kid or wife did them. But the moment *he* realized they were bad . . . that's when he became responsive." I finished my drink and left, having learned a valuable lesson.

Don't volunteer your opinion of a campaign. Instead, take the positive approach and encourage the person you're talking with to review some of your work. While at your meeting, casually get around to the ad campaign and ask how the other party feels about it. You'll find out in short order. If pressed, merely tell the person you're calling on that it's not fair for you to make an evaluation without knowing more about the product, the market direction, etc. This approach will keep you out of trouble most of the time.

Good hunting. . . .

9 Television and Radio

An advertising man who suddenly received a lot of press in the local advertising columns for getting numerous new accounts was asked how his agency could grow while others were having a hard time getting new business. His reply: "I watch television on all the odd stations and at strange hours. I listen to all the lower and upper band radio stations and I jot down the names of advertisers in my area." By calling the advertisers who bought time on odd stations at odd hours he was able to assemble a list of auto dealers, homebuilders, carpet companies, restaurants, and others whose approach to advertising was strictly amateurish. He called, arranged to meet them, and in short order walked away with the accounts.

In general, he was going after the small retailers and service people to build his billings and to create a name for himself in the business. Once his performance was established, he was in a better position to call on larger accounts . . . and get them. He handled a little over $1,500,000 in billing his first two years and added another $1,000,000 his third year. From there on, he continued to add to his billing, growing into a $5,000,000 agency in a very short time.

Now remember, though watching television and listening to the radio helped, his success came about because of a good presentation, the right kind of creative staff, and a willingness to service the accounts properly. If all you had to do to acquire new business was to watch television and listen to the radio, this book would be one chapter long. New business takes work, too!

Basically, this chapter is directed to agencies billing under $5,000,000. For those agencies, the kinds of advertisers that advertise in fringe time (other than prime time) are, for the most part, retailers of one sort or another. Their budgets can range from $7,000 per year to as high as $200,000 per year. It depends on the geographic area and the nature of the account.

Watching television and listening to the radio can be fun as well as profitable, so here are some tips on how to make this activity beneficial to your new business process.

Let's take radio first. Unlike television, there is a great deal to tune into. There are numerous AM and FM stations, some on the air twenty-four hours a day. Each offers something special to listeners and advertisers: rock, jazz, opera, classical, talk, religious, musicals, nostalgia, and country-and-western, to name a few. Again, your geographic location will determine what your local stations are doing.

If you are an early riser or a late-to-bed type, you can spend this time listening for commercial messages, which generally occur every 15 minutes, day and evening, so you don't need to stay tuned all the time.

Being in the advertising agency business gives you an opportunity to check out each station thoroughly. By calling the reps or the stations, you can secure information about the station program format, its listeners and demographics, and its policy for airing commercials. You might even be able to acquire a list of advertisers that advertise on the station. The key here is to take advantage of your profession and learn as much about each radio station as you can.

Do this, by the way, without causing any inconvenience to the station and its representatives. One sure way to get off to a bad start is to create a lot of unnecessary busy work for a station and then not get back to them. As an advertising agency, you can openly tell them you are updating your broadcast files and would like the information for that purpose. But avoid giving the station the impression you have some secret client in your pocket who is going to spend vast sums of money on that station. You'll create nothing but bad will with the station. When it comes time for a prospective client to check you out, he or she may very well go to the station for a recommendation. Guess what the station is going to say about you?

Another hazard you face by giving stations the runaround is the lack of service and cooperation when you need them. If you have caused the station unncessary grief and then you pop up with one of its accounts as your account, the station may make life miserable for you. Sure, it's easy for you to go to the new client and tell him or her all the bad things the station did, like miss a healthy portion of the flight schedule or create constant preemptions and so on. What does the station care what you say? The way they figure, they're going to get the client back one way or another. Besides, some agencies make an occupation of accusing the media about what doesn't get done. Rest assured your clients have heard it all before.

Therefore, when you do your homework, be sure you are up front with the station people. But don't tell them you are gathering all this information because you plan to solicit their advertisers. You'll get a lot of polite conversation from them but not a wealth of information. After all, why should they deal with an agency when they can deal with the client directly? And save money doing it?

This is not to say that radio stations and other media don't appreciate the job advertising agencies do. But in some cases, it's easier for them to deal directly with clients and save themselves the trouble of being in the middle. Why do you think stations have house accounts or direct accounts? And why do you have to work so hard getting the reps to give you leads to these direct accounts? Because the reps and/or the stations feel it is better to deal with the account "one-on-one." They make 15 percent more by retaining the account in their own service circles. But please remember this: Radio and television stations are represented by some of the most capable people you will ever do business with. Station management is very keen on recognizing the capabilities of the advertising agency, but sometimes the station and the advertiser prefer each other's exclusive company.

Certainly, the stations have their own reasons for retaining accounts. This chapter, however, does not deal with the stations' policies and procedures. It deals with how to get leads in spite of the stations' policies.

After you have done your homework and know what each station is all about, look at your list of stations and compare your research with reliable information concerning each station's popularity during its entire broadcasting period: Look at the listener studies in a seven-day period and at different times while the station is on the air. If the station is on twenty-four hours, look to see which are the most listened-to times and which are not. Compare this information with the station's rate card. Once this is accomplished, decide which stations are best for you to listen to. Weed out those stations that will do you little good. But remember the kinds of accounts you are going after. In some cases, the cheaper the rates, the less the potential account has to spend overall.

Look at the format of the station as well. A classical station will appeal to one kind of advertiser, whereas a rock station or a country-and-western station will appeal to another kind of client. Which kind of account do you want?

After you have your weeding out of the way, get to the listening. Keep a radio in your office and turn it on during commercial message times. Listen to your radio in the car, and again at home. After a while, you will begin to realize who is advertising more frequently and who is not. Skip around the dial and listen to other stations on your list and take notes on those accounts you believe fit your criteria for potential prospects.

Set up specific times to listen to the stations. When you have your schedule established and feel comfortable, you will be well on your way to knowing when to listen and when not. But most importantly, you will be able to approach your listening wisely without wasting a lot of time.

Television stations aren't as numerous as radio stations and, depending on where you live, you may have many to watch but not as many to pay attention to. In the television category, there are network channels and independent channels, including an assortment of UHF stations. Cable television offers some special opportunities for smaller agencies to get involved with television advertising. Generally, local cable stations have much lower advertising rates, which opens up the market to clients who can't afford the rates on "free" television.

In addition, the cable television business is based on the concept of "narrowcasting," that is, programming and advertising geared to a narrowly defined segment of the population. Single programs, or even whole channels, have been created to target specific audiences, like sports viewers, children, or women who follow fashion. These special focuses provide new outlets for agencies that specialize in certain business segments.

Each station has differences in format and in programming that make it attractive to advertisers for one reason or another. Here again, you must do your homework to determine what each station offers, at what times it offers it, and how much it costs.

Watching television is not as difficult as listening to the radio. Usually you will watch television either in the morning or in the evening after work. It may also be wise to have a television set at the office so you can monitor the channels for commercials. Generally the UHF stations will carry most of the retailers in your area, followed by the local VHF stations. Network stations will carry a heavier load of national accounts and will usually have local advertisers on during fringe times. Prime time, of course, will more than likely be sponsored by heavy national advertisers. If that's the direction you are going in . . . great. However, if you are going after local advertisers, you are better advised to concentrate on local stations.

One ad person may be able to watch television into the wee hours of the morning. But what if you are not a night owl? What if you are a regular sort who gets bleary-eyed late at night? Don't despair. Find someone to monitor commercials for you—a worker or night guard who watches TV from midnight till sunup could be the answer. Finding people to monitor TV for you and report on the commercials they watch can save you valuable time. (By the way, this method will work for radio as well.)

If you don't mind doing some editing, it's just as easy to set up your own video cassette recorder. Tape the stations and time segments that interest you. Then spend a few hours on the weekend editing the week's commercials.

Whether you record and edit the commercials yourself, or hire someone to monitor them for you, you'll need to compile a weekly report. Prepare a form with spaces for the name of the advertiser, the advertiser's phone and location, product advertised, the station the advertisement ran on, and the time of day. Inform your monitors not to duplicate their efforts. For example, if the ABC Company ran an ad on television or the radio at

10 A.M. and they recorded it, tell your monitors not to record that company's ads during the rest of the day—unless, of course, you want to gain frequency information. After a month of this monitoring, you should have a very good idea as to who is advertising when and at what times of the day. Although a monitor force can save valuable time, it is still advisable to watch TV and listen to the radio frequently yourself to get leads.

Another point. Remember the previous chapter's advice about how to tell a potential client that his or her ad was done poorly? The same rule applies here as well but with more flexibility. You can approach an advertiser and, in a sense, tell him or her you think the commercials could be better. But go lightly. A lot of radio and TV advertisers are eager to have their broadcast efforts work and are very sensitive to criticism. If you, as an advertising professional, think someone's campaign doesn't quite get the message across, the advertiser will more than likely listen to you. More often than not, the spots were done by the stations themselves. Hence, a "go lightly" approach in criticizing an ad's weak creativity may help you get the account. But again, size up your prospect first.

Don't forget that in this video age, television isn't the only place to use videotape advertisements. Many manufacturing firms produce films showing how to use their product, or how to wear it, that can be shown on a monitor in a retail store. At any trade show, crowds will gather to watch a film, and that creates excitement for the product. Another example is Nordic Trak, which markets its expensive exercise equipment directly to consumers, sends out demonstration tapes to the homes of interested buyers, so they can see the product in action.

10 Watching the Opposition

All advertising industry publications, whether local or national, report on account changes. Your local marketing column will tell you who is changing agencies or seeking to change. Changing accounts is a way of life in our business.

The average life of an account is approximately eight years. But we also know that in the world of advertising the life of an account can sometimes be measured in months, or even weeks. There are tales of agencies picking up a new piece of business on Monday and being notified a week later the account is going to another agency! If ad people have irregular heartbeats, that's one reason.

Now, before you freeze in your seat and break into a cold sweat about the accounts you're about to lose, sit back. We have discussed several viable reasons why clients leave agencies. Maybe there are clients who hire one day and fire the next, but chances are that this form of client is a rare bird and that you have been able to determine the client's idiosyncrasies early enough to warn you of this danger.

That accounts or clients do change agencies is a fact of life in the advertising business. But by the time you've finished this book, you should have a good idea about *why* clients change. Keeping tabs on account changes is a must! Here's why: A lot of advertising agencies go to extremes to get a new piece of business. While most agencies go about getting an account correctly, there are times when something is said or done that leads the prospect to believe that the agency will perform certain tasks or hire certain people or do something special in order to get the business. Though clients are skeptical, they also want to believe.

Remember, ours is a people business. A prospect judges you on what *you say you can do.* He or she listens to the verbal statements you make during the presentation. He or she looks at the visuals you show. And he or she considers a number of other factors, too. But the truth of the matter is that an account *never really gets to know the agency it hires until it works with it.* This, ladies and gentlemen, is the main reason why you want to keep up-to-date on accounts considering agency changes. Usually, a company that hires a new agency will know in six months to a year whether the relationship will work. And if it doesn't work, they're going to be looking again.

There are several problems that cause new client agency associations to break apart early. The extreme situation is if the agency goes out of business. Or an agency may merge or be bought by another agency that has conflicting accounts. There may be agency personnel changes, such as the account executive leaving to join another company as director of advertising or marketing. And the client may not be happy with the new account manager. Or a creative director or an art director may leave the agency, again prompting the newly acquired account to look elsewhere. And, finally, the agency may not deliver what it said it would, causing an early hardship for the client and putting him or her in the market for a new advertising agency.

In order to stay on top of all these potential personnel changes, it is wise to establish either a separate card file or a separate follow-up file. This is easy to do and easy to maintain. Here's how to go about it. First, we know that account changes occur every year, every month, every week. They are reported in *Advertising Age*, as well as in your local marketing column. The easiest way to keep track of personnel is to list them under their company's names on your computer files. Make a note of when the executive joined the firm, along with any background information you may have. Follow up on this news with a letter congratulating the executive on his or her new post.

If you have the time, it may be helpful to create another computer file as a cross-reference. In this file, list all the names of key executives. Write up a short biography of each one. This way, you can follow the career paths of people who are important to your business.

If you elect to set up a card file, you should purchase divider tabs arranged by the month. Next, pick or choose those accounts reportedly hiring a new agency. On a four-by-six card, write the following information: name, address, and phone number of the client company; names of the president, the ad manager, and the director of marketing; the client's product or service; annual advertising expenditures; and the name of the newly appointed agency and the official appointment date. File this card (or cards) in your card file six months ahead of the date you took the information. For example, if you fill out the card in February, file it behind the tab marked "August."

After you've done this, sit down and write the president and the advertising manager a letter of congratulation on the hiring of your competitor. (See Appendix A, Example 10.) End your letter by stating your interest in meeting with the client should it be necessary. If, after a year or a year and a half of casual follow-up, nothing happens, file the card in the inactive section of your other card file.

The alternative to this procedure is the follow-up file. This method of staying abreast of account changes can be productive, but awkward to use. Here again, you write a letter of congratulation to the president and the advertising manager. Make a copy and note the month (again, six months ahead) in which you are to follow up. Be sure you keep this file organized. If you don't, you'll find important follow-up dates are missed. That's the problem with a letter follow-up file. Though you have two choices, I recommend the card file system.

Stay alert, keep your cards organized, and this procedure will work for you. It's a long-term investment of time, but one that has paid off for other agencies.

⬛⬛⬛ Rubbing Elbows for Fun and Profit

Rubbing elbows by joining clubs, associations, and organizations can be profitable. This form of social detective work has aided many a new business executive in acquiring valuable leads and invitations to meet with key people in various companies and corporations.

The following story is just one example of the importance of being a joiner.

A small advertising agency in Chicago decided to go after clients in a specific industry—homebuilding (a lucrative opportunity if you know what you're doing). After all, they figured, they knew the industry and would know what the problems and opportunities were. So, they set out to capture as many accounts in that industry as they could.

The agency's executives combed the local and metro newspapers every Monday calling homebuilders that had advertised the week before, an average of 200 to 300 advertisements per week. After a year of cold phone calls, the agency had acquired about six new accounts—not a very good figure, considering the wealth of clients that existed.

Nonetheless, they continued. Then one morning one of their clients called and asked that one of the principals of the agency attend a seminar being conducted by the Greater Chicago Home Builders Association. The client couldn't make it but paid for the ticket. The seminar was on marketing and advertising, so the agency principal went.

Not only was the agency head impressed with the content of the seminar but even more with the list of members who represented many of the homebuilders in the Chicago area. During a cocktail party after the seminar, the agency principal met many prospective accounts and, later, through contacts made at the seminar, was invited to pitch two homebuilder accounts. The agency got both accounts. Later on, the agency joined the association and in four years added more homebuilder clients and became a leader in homebuilder marketing and advertising. By joining the association, the agency became better known, more knowledgeable about potential accounts, and healthier from a profit standpoint. Moral: If you haven't considered clubs, organizations, and associations, you should.

By joining, you will come in contact with many decision-making people who could very well become your new clients. Think for a moment about how many different kinds of groups there are and how important being a member can be.

Associations. Most, if not all, segments of business and industry have an association. Associations provide a wealth of services and advice for their dues-paying members. If you specialize in an industry such as finance, agriculture, medicine, or travel (to name a few), becoming a member of the industry's key association can be very beneficial to you. You'll meet potential accounts, gain valuable knowledge, and become better known within that industry.

Association membership, likewise, can be extremely helpful if you have a particularly important client and feel the association will help you build a better client relationship. If, unfortunately, you lose the account, you will have amassed enough good will to acquire another, similar account. It has happened!

Clubs. Clubs are usually more social in nature than associations. There are all sorts of clubs—advertising clubs, country clubs, health clubs, travel clubs, investment clubs, card clubs, gourmet clubs, gun clubs, stamp clubs, antique clubs, auto clubs—the list goes on and on.

Try to remember, however, that you have only so much time

during the average week or month to participate in club functions. If you're spread too thin by being an active member of too many clubs, you'll defeat your purpose as well as waste a lot of money and time. Therefore be judicious in your selection. Join clubs that you can benefit from, not only from the vantage point of new business, but socially as well. If you hate bridge, don't join the local community bridge club just because you think you can get new business. You'll be bored to death. But do join a backgammon club if you have even a slight interest in the subject and if, more importantly, you can meet people worthwhile to you in your new business effort.

In other words, take an inventory of your likes and interests and match them to the clubs that offer you an opportunity to have fun and an opportunity to meet important people at the same time. Remember, club membership costs money in the form of dues. If there are several clubs that provide you with the criteria mentioned, have the agency pick up the tab. It's conceivable this expense is tax-deductible. Consult with your company attorney or accountant. But more important, the cost will pay for itself in the long run. Join as many clubs as you feasibly can in terms of time.

Organizations. Let's consider organizations just in the areas of politics and charity. These two types of organizations afford you a great opportunity for meeting senior executives, well-known individuals, and politicians. Being actively involved in politics and charity functions is a good way to get an ongoing flow of publicity, too. Most importantly you will meet prominent people who will be for the most part chief executive officers of major corporations. What better way to get new business than to be chummy with the upper echelon of some of America's top corporations?

Getting "in" is the key to this proposition. It isn't easy! But here are a few tips that should help. Read the society columns in your area. Find out who is the chairperson of each of the more prominent charitable organizations. Write each a letter telling him or her what great work the organization is doing and how the chairperson is to be commended for his or her efforts. End the letter by volunteering to get involved in one form or another. Publicity would be right up your alley.

Then sit back and hope the phone rings or a reply comes in the mail. Should you not receive a reply, the next best thing to do is to rent a tuxedo and attend the organization's functions. While there, arrange in one way or another to meet some of the organization's key people. Express your desire to get involved in the work. Later, follow up your conversation with a brief thank-you note and re-affirmation of your interest. In short order, you should be involved to your heart's content. Warning: Don't be overbearing in your attempt to become one of the elite. You'll only be regarded with suspicion. Go slowly, but steadily.

After you've chosen several clubs, organizations, and associations to join, be an *active* member. Be enthusiastic. In time, as the other members get to know you better, you'll begin to acquire valuable new business leads and invitations.

▐12▌ Going Shopping

Shopping for what, you ask? Shopping for leads to new accounts. If you live and work in a large metropolitan area, you are probably surrounded by every variety of store and every variety of product known. No matter what you want, you'll probably find it in Chicago, Los Angeles, New York, Atlanta, or any large populated area.

But shopping for products per se is not what we're talking about in this chapter; shopping for clients is. To client-shop, arm yourself with a pad of paper and pen and get set to visit some stores. As an example, let's take an imaginary walk through a supermarket. First, get a cart to walk around with. Supermarket managers get nervous and ask questions if all you are doing is walking around with a pad of paper and a pen. They think you're the competition checking on prices.

Now walk down any aisle and you'll notice the difference in shelf space allotments. For instance, if you are near the shelves with rice packages, you'll notice that Minute Rice or Uncle Ben's has more product facings than less popular brands. This is because the store sells more of these branded products than the XYZ brand that has a single facing. The store is probably storing greater quantities of Uncle Ben's and Minute Rice than XYZ rice and the store manager has been sold on the fact that these two leaders will support their product with consumer advertising, which in turn, will cause more of the product to be sold.

Any aisle of a store will reveal the difference in product facings. The one with the most facings is the product leader. The product with the least facings is "following the leader." Think of any product and you'll find this rule applies.

The new business trick in this regard is to jot down the names, addresses, and product descriptions of the manufacturers with fewer facings than the leaders on your pad. Note, too, the competition in that product area. You can do this in almost any department except the meat area and the fresh produce section.

Next, when your list of "weak" products is complete, do some research to determine who each manufacturer is. Try to find out how the product is distributed—nationally, seminationally, regionally, and so on.

Find out who the advertising manager is. After you've developed a profile of each manufacturer, call the ad manager. (Try to get his or her name in advance.) Tell the advertising manager you've seen the company's product and that you would like to come over and explain how your advertising agency can develop a program that may increase the consumer awareness of the product, boost stores' awareness of it, and gain additional shelf space in those stores. More than likely, you'll get an audience.

Of course you can't solve all the underdog's problems. Some companies you may not even want to approach, for a variety of reasons. Remember also that some companies are at full production capacity and the one thing they don't need is advertising. However, you will need to call and correspond with these companies to understand fully their opportunities and objectives.

Do your store checks every six months. By doing this, you'll stay abreast of products new to the market and those that have failed in the market. We have shown you how to take a tour through a supermarket. But shopping for the weaker products can take place in a variety of stores, such as drugstores, toy stores, clothing stores, hardware stores, lawn and garden stores, record stores, bookstores, discount stores, cookware stores, sporting goods stores, jewelry stores, and so on.

Establish your own criteria about the kind of products for which you would like to do the advertising. If your preference is food, obviously hardware stores will not fit the bill. If all varieties of stores, on the other hand, fit your plan, then you must pace yourself, since shopping is a fun but exhausting activity.

13 The Library—It's Free

Wouldn't it be nice if you had in your home all the books relative to product research, all the demographic breakdowns, all the periodicals, the periodical digests, histories of companies, and, in general, the necessary reference materials to help you get leads and thoroughly check them out? Wouldn't it be nice to have a wealth of business books so you could accurately predict changes in society and trends?

Well, if you had all of the material mentioned above and then some, you would need an addition built onto your house. Worse, it would cost you a fortune to maintain this collection. And inasmuch as most new business executives don't have an easy $1,000,000 or $2,000,000 to build such a space, the best thing available to you is your local library.

Libraries are like products. They come in a variety of systems, sizes, shapes, and services. Some are much better than others. Certainly the best way to determine how *your* library fares is to visit it and examine it. Become fully acquainted with its departments, its volume of resources, its policies and procedures. Ask the chief librarian for a tour of the facility. After all, the staff is there to make the library work for you.

In a moment, we'll look at why a library is important to your new business pursuits. But for now, let's see how to "check out" your library.

Read the library's bulletin board and look for lecture notices.

Look over the reference department closely. See if the library is current in its selection of newly published material. Ask if the library is part of a cooperative exchange program so that if you need a book or other material, it can be easily borrowed from a nearby library. See if the library receives all of the local, state, and federal bulletins and announcements. Check to see if they have an annual report file. How many magazines and varieties of newspapers do they have? Are past issues of magazines and newspapers filed away or microfilmed? These are a few questions you will want answers to. But as your familiarity with the library grows, you may have other questions based on your needs.

Once you have determined the full extent of your library, its pros and cons, check other libraries in your area. Again, all libraries are basically the same but there are differences and it's a good policy to be familiar with several libraries. This way, if you *need* something and your local library does not have it, you can check with other libraries close by.

Next rule: Make a habit of spending at least an hour a week at the library. Some executives prefer going to the library on a weekday evening after dinner, while others stay away from the library at this time because of the many students who use the library for school work. Generally, the best time to go is a weekend afternoon because new materials from the previous week have been filed and are available. And usually the library is quieter and calmer.

The library is free unless you abuse the loaning privilege and owe for overdue books. At the library, you can keep abreast of current trends, personnel changes, business developments, and governmental happenings. Each of these subjects affects the advertising community. However, the main area where you will want to concentrate your efforts is the periodical department. Here again, and depending on the size of your library, you will find an array of magazines, newspapers, and newsletters to read through. Choose the periodicals that will offer you the most information on leads and current developments.

Here's a story that may provide you with a bit more incentive to spend time in the periodical department. The executive vice president of an agency billing $10,000,000 was responsible for new business development. In his pursuit of new accounts, he discovered the library. He was elated when he realized the wealth of information in this facility. Every Sunday at noon he would find a comfortable easy chair in the periodical department, arrange his selection of freshly chosen magazines and newspapers into a neat pile and proceed to read. With pad of paper and pen in hand, he would take note of executive changes, mergers, reported profit losses, trends, newly formed companies and corporations, and new product announcements.

One weekend, while reading a trade publication whose contents dealt with the lawn and garden business, he stumbled on a small news release about a unique, new product that a company had recently begun producing. So small was the story that he would have easily overlooked it had he not been careful to scrutinize each page. After his session in the periodical department, he took his notes to the reference department to continue his investigation of the companies he had listed. One thing led to another and the following Monday he called the company that made the new lawn and garden implement. He was invited out for a conversation. Six meetings and a presentation later, he and his agency picked up a new $1,000,000 account.

The executive said later that the publication from which he got the lead was one he had never heard of before and he doubts he would have had access to the publication at the agency.

What does this story tell you? It should tell you that a constant, ongoing relationship with the library, especially the periodical department, can mean, without a doubt, new business opportunities.

The reference department of your library is a good source of research material as well. After gaining valuable, fresh information from the periodicals department (your starting point), use the reference department to do some needed homework and research. If you come across an executive change announcement, the reference department will help you find information on the company. The reference department will probably have the current *Standard Directory of Advertisers* (Red Book), with which you should be familiar. They'll have the *Standard Directory of Advertising Agencies* and the *Thomas Register*. They also may have all the *Who's Who* books and the Dun and Bradstreet reports.

The reference department maintains reference material you may never have thought would be available. Here again, get acquainted with this department. Know what is offered. You'll be glad you did because, needless to say, the more you know about a prospect the better off you're going to fare during the selection process.

In Appendix B of this book there is a selection of useful reference material that you can look for in your local library.

14 The Yellow Pages and Other Directories

To many, cold-calling is what a door-to-door salesperson does to earn a living. We ad folk feel that cold-calling is beneath us and so we don't practice what can be a profitable form of salesmanship. Yet cold-calling is a must in the lineup of lead-getting tools. Although you have an arsenal of ways to get leads and new business, cold-calling is, by far, the most expedient form.

There are basically three ways of cold-calling: by phone, by mail, and by personally knocking on doors. To be successful at cold-calling, you must be scientific in your approach and develop a list of companies along with their ad managers, marketing directors, or presidents. In order to develop your list, you need a source to work from. That's where the Yellow Pages and other directories enter.

Let's begin by discussing some of the directories that will be of most value to you. For the advertising business, the best directory to have is the *Standard Directory of Advertisers,* either geographical or categorical. This directory is published annually by The National Register Publishing Company (5201 Old Orchard Road, Skokie, Illinois 60076). It lists some 17,000 advertisers. Each entry gives the company name, address, phone number, total number of employees, total sales, key personnel by title, annual advertising and market allocation, present advertising agency, and a media breakdown for the advertising allocation. This book is by far the most utilized by new business hunters.

Another valuable directory is the *Thomas Register,* which essentially lists the same information, except for the marketing and advertising monetary breakdown.

For a far less detailed listing of companies in a particular field either in your area or other areas—and a publication often overlooked as a potential source—use the Yellow Pages. Many new business executives who deal on a local level use the Yellow Pages to list important companies in several categories for cold-calling. New business leads can also be gathered this way.

There are many other directories to choose from. Here again, the reference department of your library should maintain quite an assortment. You'll find directories listing franchises, banks, savings and loans, travel agents, chefs and restaurants, publishers, drug and chemical manufacturers, governmental agencies, and many others. You be the judge as to the best source for you.

Once you have pared down your list of directories, start to use them by acquiring as much useful information about new business prospects as you can. Transfer your information to a computer file, or to four-by-six cards, listing company name, address, phone number, products, annual sales, ad manager, ad budget, and present agency. Be aware that most directories, other than the *Directory of Advertisers,* do not provide you with advertising budgets or the name of the advertising director. Some of this information you will need to gather through other methods.

You should keep these four-by-six cards separate from your other cards. Most of the cards you have already filled out represent stronger leads, whereas the cards you collect from directories should be designated cold-call cards. Generally cold-call cards are used when you have some spare time to develop new leads.

Based on the other methods available to you, cold-calling can be an important, last-resort effort. Agencies do generate leads and new business from this method. But remember, cold-calling is the most difficult and the most frustrating of all the tools you have. More often than not, you will need a good phone voice and a good phone procedure. Some believe you must make as many as twenty-five calls to produce a decent new business nibble.

Your ratio of calls to viable contacts depends on you. But the point of this brief chapter is to tell you *not* to overlook the use of directories for developing another important list.

15 Self Promotion

Letters and direct mail go hand-in-hand. But the question remains: Do advertising, direct mail, and letters promote your agency effectively enough to generate interest on the part of the companies and the corporations that receive them to take notice of your agency and its abilities?

This is a tough question to answer but one that needs to be addressed. There are advertising agencies in the United States that swear by self promotion. And, there are advertising agencies that will tell you not to waste your time and money. Yet most agencies believe that advertising, direct mail, and letter campaigns do make the agency "noticeable."

"If your efforts produce no response," reported one agency executive, "they will at least help you open a few doors when you follow up by phone." He went on to say that nothing gets you access quicker than to say you are calling because of a letter you wrote. You will almost always get to talk to someone.

If self promotion infallibly produced concrete sales results, everyone would be doing it. As it is, many agencies like to advertise to keep their agency name familiar. And again, many agencies combine tactics and use a direct mail campaign both as a vehicle to keep their name familiar and as a tool for follow-up. Let's look at some successful efforts.

A small agency in the Midwest seeking to acquire new retail accounts secured a list of retailers in its area and sent a mailing to each, offering to conduct a free evaluation of the retailer's advertising and marketing effort. The mailer indicated that agency executives would come out and evaluate the retailer's premises, its employees, and the retailer's competition. The agency sent 1,000 pieces of mail, received ten inquiries, and, from that, acquired two new accounts. Note the procedure: making the results of a privately conducted study available or offering something special generally produces the best response.

Businesses often produce their own newsletters, which they send to clients on a regular basis. In this way, they let clients know that the agency is interested and involved in new developments in the industry. At the same time, the newsletter keeps the agency's name in front of the client.

Another small agency conducted a mailing to a list of potential accounts but, realizing from past experience that many of their letters and mailed materials were filed by the prospective account in a special file marked "agency solicitations," the agency sent their mailing in a red file with the tab printed to read "Agency Solicitation by the XYZ Agency." The agency reportedly has a lot of red files located in the filing cabinets of prospective accounts. But there is no word yet as to whether they picked up any new business.

Often an agency uses advertising specialties to draw attention to its name. Imprinted ad specialties run the gamut from ballpoint pens, to ash trays, coffee mugs, and calendars. One executive affirmed that this form of promotion serves one essential need: to keep the agency's name always out front.

Some agencies print and mail interesting posters, alerting their prospects to good work accomplished or good people they employ who do the work. This is an interesting way to get attention, but poster mailings have problems. For one thing, they're hard to file and as a result tend to get thrown away. A word to the wise should be sufficient.

Most agencies send letters and profiles of the agency to prospects. This technique often provides them with new business leads and many agencies consider it the best approach.

Agencies frequently send letters to prospects with freshly printed examples of their work. This is effective as well.

And, last but not least, some agencies go to a great deal of trouble creating and printing brochures and special material to entice new business prospects. Some packages work; others don't.

As you can imagine, all sorts of goodies are sent in the mail in the hopes of evoking a positive reaction. It is really hard to tell what works and what doesn't. An evaluation of your prospect file should help you determine the proper steps to take. You may decide *not* to do a mailing. And then again, you may find a mailing to be very beneficial to your cause.

As for advertising, you are your own best or worst client. Being in the advertising business, you have available the necessary tools to determine if you should advertise yourself. Evaluate yourself as a client. Analyze the cost effectiveness of a mass communication effort versus the other methods listed in this book.

Don't do what a lot of agencies do: simply run an ad blindly or haphazardly put out a mailing thinking that *you,* of all people, will gain a greater exposure and response because *you're* in the advertising business. Would you forge ahead for one of your clients without a proper ad plan? No! Since you wouldn't use this approach for your client, you shouldn't use it for yourself.

Prepare a campaign for your own business, including a budget, timetable, and target audience. Do some background research so you'll know just how extensive you want the campaign to be.

Weigh all the pluses and minuses. You may determine that self promotion would be futile. Then again, you may discover that certain forms of promotion are better for you than for others. But, by all means, do some *homework.* Know thyself!

Go ahead, mail a couple of times a year. Run some ads . . . but do it only if it's right and do it well and do it professionally. Remember, too, you're selling professional, creative communication. The very first impression a prospect gets of you is what he or she sees in an ad or receives in the mail. That impression must be the *best* you can make.

16 What to Do When You Get the Lead

You've done your homework, organized your cards, been religious about follow-up, and canvassed your friends and associates for tips.

Now, finally, the big lead comes. What next?

Answering questions about how to proceed would take another book. But there are a few questions that come up more frequently than others. Here are some random suggestions about how to handle a lead once you get it.

1. Whom do you call to get an appointment? There are those who will tell you always to call or write the director of advertising. And there are those who will tell you to contact the marketing director. Since advertising comes under marketing, the marketing director supposedly is responsible for the advertising decision. Then, there are those who will swear up and down that the president of the company should be approached first. Confusing and contradictory advice, without a doubt—isn't it?

Let's clarify it for you. First of all, *most* companies and corporations are like the military. They have a chain of command that starts with the chairman of the board and ends, usually, with the mail clerk. Each link in the chain is an autonomous command center, meaning each manager has troops to whom he or she delegates authority. Smaller companies and corporations—and smaller divisions within a large company—are the exception to the rule in that one person is often responsible for several widely varying tasks.

Just the same, there is a top and a bottom to every company or corporate totem pole. Whom you call on depends largely on the makeup and stature of the corporation you're calling. For instance, if you want to call General Motors, it's unlikely that the corporate president will have the time or desire to talk to you, especially since General Motors has several divisions operated autonomously by division presidents. Next, almost certainly, the president of General Motors is more concerned with the overall profit and loss picture of the corporation and has entrusted the advertising and marketing to the divisional managers. They, in turn, have divisional marketing and advertising directors reporting to them, while they—the division presidents—keep track of day-to-day operational activities. Hence, for this size of corporation, you will probably be better off contacting each division's marketing and advertising managers. This way, you'll save yourself a great deal of time.

Now, let's assume you've realistically assembled a good new business plan. You're already aware that a select few advertising agencies are qualified to approach a corporation the size of General Motors. Regardless, if you feel there may be an opportunity to solicit some business, go for it. The point of this explanation is that the bigger the company and/or corporation, the less your chances are of talking to the chief executive officer. The best rule of thumb about whom to approach is *always* the key decision-maker, the one who is going to sign your contract. That can be, depending on the company, the director of advertising or the president.

Start at the top. Try to establish contact with the chief executive officer first. If that fails, then contact the person directly responsible to top management for the advertising function. This may well be the advertising manager. Though the advertising manager may not have the authority to sign you up, he or she may have the ear of the person who does. At best, this approach will give you an opportunity to discover who the real authorities are. In other words, you may learn a lot even if you don't get in to see the president.

Remember again that the larger conglomerates have divisions or subsidiaries. Instead of going right to the top of the corporate structure, approach the division or subsidiary leaders and/or their advertising people first.

It is important that you don't step on any toes in pursuit of an account. This can be done when you send a letter to the president and he or she sends it to the director of advertising for follow-up. The ad director will think you don't recognize his or her position of authority since you obviously believe he or she is not worth contacting. Getting an appointment is going to be tough from this point on!

Likewise, if you get the president on the phone, more than likely, he or she will instruct you to contact the director of advertising. Yes, the president may be interested in your story but, by the same token, he or she has a delegation of authority to protect. Whatever you do, don't get on the phone with the ad director and say that the president said you ought to talk to him or her. This technique is sure to cause problems.

Conclusion: It is advisable that you initiate contact with both parties simultaneously. This way, you won't hurt any feelings.

2. Is homework valuable? Yes! If one has a solid lead, a new business practitioner enhances his or her position by contacting the appropriate person, establishing a time to meet, and gathering as much information about the prospect as possible. This way you can be somewhat intelligent about your prospect's problems or opportunities. Doing homework and having good information can often turn a chilly agency pitch into a positive, meaningful conversation, and just maybe, into a new account.

3. What about entertainment? Does it help? Is it getting out of control? Sometimes inexperienced people can overwine and dine a new business prospect. Generally, you should consider entertaining a prospective client when dealing with the prospect in his or her own office would be distracting and awkward. So, you take him or her to lunch or dinner. By removing the prospect from a busy environment, you can get down to business.

But don't go overboard. You can turn a prospect off by constantly coming up with invitations to cocktail parties, football games, and so on. Most prospects feel uncomfortable with these proposals and would rather deal with you on a business basis. Some prospects even grow suspicious of lunch invitations. The only time to invite a prospect to functions and dinner out is if the chemistry between you is real and not imagined. Entertainment can be pleasant, but it is peripheral to business.

4. What about a cocktail party for prospects only? It's been tried many times. The general feeling is that if you get a room full of prospects together three things will happen: (a) they will probably stand around and talk to each other, (b) the wrong agency person may say or do the wrong thing, and (c) most prospects like to think you are romancing them exclusively. Put one prospect in a room with other prospects, and he or she will begin to wonder what's wrong with the agency that it must put forth a blitz effort for accounts. Probably all the prospects will have a good time (of sorts), but you're still going to have to deal with them one at a time at a later date. Why spend the money for food and booze and a lavish party if you're only going to duplicate the effort later for each individual?

No, don't have a party for all your prospects. Save the money instead for a crackerjack presentation for each, individually.

5. How do you write a letter that will produce an audience? How much mail do you get a day at the office and at home? If you are like most people, you get a good amount.

How much of it do you open and immediately throw away? Probably a lot.

But what about the mail you get from unknown sources that you read thoroughly? Or better, respond to. What is it that seizes your attention? The difference rests in the approach. It also rests in the mailer's ability to put himself or herself on the receiving end.

Let's begin by understanding some basic realities. Whatever you send stands as the first impression the prospect will have of you and your agency. Next, most of the people you want to write to are very, very busy. They can't possibly read everything that comes in. And lastly, the first paragraph of the letter will either make it or break it for you!

Let's say you want to write the advertising manager and the president of a company that has expressed an interest in talking to advertising agencies. You learned about them through a lead you acquired. They are senior executives *who don't know you.* Their time is valuable and they have many important things to do. In all probability, their secretaries read and screen their mail, only passing on letters and communications that are important and tossing the rest or passing it on to junior executives. You want a reply in the form of an appointment by way of a return letter or phone call. Here's how you proceed:

- Be sure you are writing to a person who exists. If your lead source gave you the person's name and title, then you're OK. If, on the other hand, you have only a company name and you check the *Directory of Advertisers* for the president's name and that of the advertising director, it is advisable that you call the company to verify the names and the address.
- Have your secretary mark the envelope "Personal and Confidential" and underscore this in red.
- Keep your letter short, but to the point.
- Don't hesitate to use a person's first name in the salutation, unless your letter is more formal and conservative, in which case you should use Mr. or Ms.
- Ask the reader to do something in return, such as write or call you back.
- Tell the reader you will follow up and will call or come by on a particular day. This approach will prompt a quick response.

Examples 11, 12, and 13 in Appendix A are letters that should bring results. They are just to give you an idea, so don't use them exactly as you see them. Instead, draft your own series of letters in the same vein as these.

6. Are finders fees legitimate? Not unless you want to be referred to as the agency that "pays off." Finders fees are probably not illegal. (You'd have to ask your agency lawyer to be sure.) But for the most part, you should believe that if a person gives you a lead, he or she is doing so because that person likes you and respects the integrity of the agency, not because he or she is going to get money for the effort.

This is not to say that finders fees are not used. However, you would probably be better off not "paying off." It will eventually hurt your reputation as well as that of the agency.

On the other hand, if you want to acknowledge a lead provided to you by someone, why not invite him or her out to dinner, or offer a ticket to a football game? Perhaps remembering the person's birthday will have the same positive effect. Trust is the key word in this respect. Not money.

14 Is This the End?

As far as getting leads to new business opportunities is concerned, you are just beginning. This book provides you with a working guide to getting bona fide new business leads. Use the suggestions to your advantage. Use some of them, parts of them, or all of them.

What you really want to know are the ways to get reliable information about a company or corporation that might seriously consider giving its advertising objectives and budget to an advertising agency. How you get beyond the first meeting and eventually to the presentation stage has to depend on you and your staff. We all know that each advertising agency has a separate personality and its approach plan will be dictated by many elements, such as size of the staff, type of accounts presently being serviced, age, reputation, and so on.

There is plenty of new business just waiting to be added to your agency list. You're going to be thoroughly amazed, and perhaps a lot wealthier, once you get organized and on the way. Now close the book—be sure you keep it close by for easy reference—and get going. Some of your new clients are waiting for you to call!

Appendix A
Examples of Records
and Letters

Example 1
Sample Memo

Dear Staff,

The agency is presently approaching several new pieces of business. We trust our efforts will ultimately produce a couple of new accounts in the near future.

One of the potential accounts is a manufacturer of petroleum by-products. Another is in the tax service business. And the third is a major distributor of a liquor product.

We'll keep you posted as to further developments. Just thought you'd like to know.

Example 2
Prospect Card

(Front)

Blue Beverage Company
1418 Allan Street   (415) 000-0000
Georgetown, MN 00000

Mfg. of Soft Drinks: Fiesta, Snappy Orange

Richard Blue—Pres.   (Sue Fields)
David Manner—Mkt. Dir.   (Karen)
Mary Green—Ad. Mgr.   (Barb)

Agency: Gregory, Black & Crawford
Budget: $1,250,000 (as of 1/16/87)

(Back)

Called 6/5/88—Talked with M. Green.
To CB 7/18/88.
Clips on file. Light research on file.

Letter 6/5/88—Follow-up to phone call, with
agency profile.

Letter 7/3/88—With/clip info.

Called 7/18/88—First meeting scheduled for
7/24/88.

Example 3
Prospect Profile

Name of company:	BLUE BEVERAGE COMPANY
Address:	1418 Allan Street Georgetown, MN 00000
Phone:	(415) 000-0000
Contact name/title:	Ms. Mary Green Ad. Manager/PR Manager
Additional names:	Richard Blue—President David Manner—Mkt. Mgr. Ken Williams—Sales Mgr. Anne Carter—Sec.
Budget:	(Est) $1,250,000
Product/service:	Fiesta Ginger Ale Snappy Orange Grumpy Grape Sparkles Spring Water
Competition:	High Life Beverage Co. Brown Cow Co. Anderson Soft Drink Corp.
Distribution area:	*Midwest:* Illinois, Wisconsin, Minnesota, Indiana, Michigan, Iowa (primary) *East Coast:* New York, New Jersey Note: Some European Dist., England, Ireland, Finland

Type of sales force: *Midwest:* Corporation salespeople (11 men, 1 woman)
East Coast: Barney & Jones (Mfg. Reps)
Europe: British Beverage Distributors, Ltd.

Agency of record: Gregory, Black & Crawford
1515 Gravel Road
Mora, MN 00000

Notes: Product has little facing in the stores. Liquor stores carry product as a low-price filler. All stores use product as a loss leader. Consumer not very familiar with product. Packaging change should be considered as well as in-store programs. (See media and special promotions notes this file.)

Example 4
House List

Melvin Arkus
505 Greenway Avenue
Arlington Heights, IL 00000
(312) 000-0000

Uncle. Sales representative for Good Life Insurance
Company. Deals mostly at corporate level.

Ann Marie Kellog
1710 Spruce Street
Algonquin, IL 00000
(312) 000-0000

Attorney and friend of wife. Does mostly corporate
work, especially helping new corporations.

Doug Foster
601 Trail Park Drive
Barrington, IL 00000
(312) 000-0000

Neighbor. Works as airline pilot. Brother president
of American Wire. Works in Cedarville, Iowa.

Example 5
Date Book

Monday, Jan. 25 _25_	Tuesday, Jan. 26 _26_
8	**8**
⑨ CALL MEL HOWARD	**9**
775-5151	
CALL MR. KRON — PRES.	
0 WILSON SKI CORP	⑩ 1ST MEETING WITH
665-0103 FOR APPT	CROWN CORP
	MR. BRUCE
1 CALL ART KENNEY AT	**11**
DUBCO FOR 2ND MEET	
⑪ 323-0518	
12 LUNCH w/ SUSAN BROWN	⑫ LUNCH WITH AD MGR OF
SEW-N-SEW MAGAZINE	GLIB RECORDS
	ANDY CARLSON
① WRITE UP PROSPECT	**1**
PROFILES	
② FOLLOW UP ON	② CALL ON PROSPECT
CARDS TODAY FOR	ACTIVE CARDS
APPOINTMENTS	
④ GET FOLLOW UP	
LETTERS DONE	
⑤	⑤
6	**6**

Example 6
Prospect Flowchart
for Files

Once the lead is transmitted,
↓
place the information on your 4″ × 6″ card.
↓
Automatically file the card behind the tab marked prospect active.
↓
After you have "worked the card," place it behind the appropriate tab (i.e., prospect inactive, follow-up, or in process).
↓
If the card is filed in follow-up or in-process:
↓
1. Write the prospect and make necessary notes;
↓
2. Place a copy of letter in three-ring notebook;
↓
3. Place additional copies in correspondence out and prospect active files; and
↓
4. Meet with the prospect.
↓
Upon gaining positive results, write up a prospect profile and place it, along with letter from follow-up notebook and prospect active file, into new file with prospect name.
↓
Prepare for presentation.

Example 7
Prospect Flowchart
for Computer

Once the lead is transmitted,
↓
enter the data on a computer file, in
alphabetical order, by last name.
↓
Use the highlight key to indicate that
the prospect is active.
↓
After you have "worked the card," put a letter code
at the beginning of the entry, indicating F for
followed-up or I for in-process.
↓
Write the prospect, and make
necessary notes.
↓
Place a copy of the letter in three-ring
notebook.
↓
Note on computer file that letter has been sent. Keep
prospect on active status.
↓
Meet with prospect.
↓
If meeting is positive, update notes.
↓
Prepare for presentation.

Example 8
Rep List

Name	Company	Product	Dept.	Sells to Agency
Dick Laker	Agri-News	Media	Media	✔
Ron Clayton	Promotions Unltd.	Premiums	Acct. Exec.	✔
Harry Bloom	ABC Typesetting	Type	Art	✔
Ann Miller	Free-lance	Copy	Creative	
Bill Sanders	That's Fine	Film Prod.	Creative	
Aaron Moore	Corner Office Supply	Office Supplies	Office Mgr.	✔

Example 9
Sample Letter to Client

September 4, 1988

Mr. Richard Blue
President
Blue Beverage Company
1418 Allan Street
Georgetown, MN 00000

Dear Dick:

   As you know, you are a valued client of this
agency, and we are proud to be a part of your
management team.

   If it's convenient, I'd like to get together with
you to talk about trends in the beverage business,
and to touch base on some other matters.

   I'll call you on September 11 to schedule a lunch
date.

Very truly yours,

Example 10
Congratulatory Letter

February 10, 1988

Mr. Norman Astor
President
Bond Adhesive Corporation
441 North Elm Street
Baylor, Indiana 00000

Dear Mr. Astor:

Although we haven't had a chance to meet, I'm familiar with your company and its business.

I and the staff of the Meis and Romando Advertising Agency want to congratulate you on your selection of the Morton, Arthur and Miller Advertising Agency. They are a very capable, highly creative group.

Likewise, our agency is capable of creating effective advertising for your products. I would like to meet with you and show you some examples of our work. At some point, you might be able to use our services.

Please allow me to call you in a day or two.

Very truly yours,

Example 11
Letter to Prospect—1

January 15, 1989

Mr. Norman Astor
President
Bond Adhesive Corporation
441 North Elm Street
Baylor, Indiana 00000

Dear Norm:

Some important information about Bond-O Glue has come to my attention, and I'd like to share it with you.

I know how busy you are, but I think we could both benefit from a brief meeting.

I'll call your secretary early next week to arrange for an appointment.

Very truly yours,

Example 12
Letter to Prospect—2

September 25, 1988

Mr. Norman Astor
President
Bond Adhesive Corporation
441 North Elm Street
Baylor, Indiana 00000

Dear Mr. Astor:

Last year I wrote a letter similar to this one to the president of The Apply-More Paint Company. In part, here's what I said and here's why we got their advertising business:

"Give me one chance to show you how well we know your business and especially an opportunity to demonstrate several ideas we created to sell more of your products."

I'm going to ask you for the same chance. But I'm going to do it with a promise. . . . I promise to take just 30 minutes and no more. If I haven't sufficiently proven to you how effective our agency can be on your behalf, I'll "fold my tent" and trouble you no further.

Unless I hear otherwise, I'll be at your office on October 5th at 10:00 a.m. promptly.

Very truly yours,

Example 13
Letter to Prospect—3

October 1, 1988

Mr. Norman Astor
President
Bond Adhesive Corporation
441 North Elm Street
Baylor, Indiana 00000

Dear Mr. Astor:

   As a major player in the industry, you probably know that last year, eight out of ten households bought some type of glue. Consumers spent a little more than one billion dollars on adhesive products. And that's not all. Industry spent an additional 750 million dollars on glue products.

   But, do you know how to get a better share of this market for Bond Adhesive Corporation? Is selling more product and increasing your revenues important to you?

   Will you see me for 30 minutes on Tuesday, October 10, at 9:30 a.m.? I've got something to discuss with you.

                                        Very truly yours,

Appendix B
Advertising Information
Resources

Associations
Networking works. Check your local Yellow Pages under "Associations" to find out which groups meet in your area. There are general organizations, such as the Advertising Women of New York, as well as more specialized groups, like the Automotive Advertisers' Council. Also look for organizations that relate to your client's business.

Books
For books on advertising, check your public library's copy of *Books in Print* in the reference section. There are hundreds of books on advertising currently in publication.

Magazines
Advertising Age
AdWeek

Advertising Directories
AdWeek Directory of Advertising. Five directories cover East, Southeast, Midwest, Southwest. 1986. B. Klein Pubs.
Advertising Career Directory: 24 Top Industry Leaders. Career Pr. Inc. [Annual]
National Directory of Product Publicity Sources, 1987. Asher-Gallant.

Standard Directory of Advertisers. National Register Publishing Company.

General Directories

Hudson's Newsletter Directory. Hudson Publications.
Thomas Register (lists companies and their lines of business).